CHAPTER 36

36 Days to Reflect & Listen

Allowing the Lord
to Speak through His Word

Erika Hartfield

Chapter 36: 36 Days to Reflect & Listen
Copyright © 2026 Erika Hartfield. All rights reserved.
No part of this publication may be reproduced, stored in a retrieval system, or transmitted in any way, by any means, whether electronically, mechanically, via photocopy, recording, or otherwise, without the prior written permission of the publisher, except as provided by USA copyright law. Thank you for your support of the author's rights.

Scripture quotations marked NIV are taken from the Holy Bible, New International Version® NIV®. Copyright © 1973, 1978, 1984, 2011 by Biblica, Inc.™ Used by permission of Zondervan. All rights reserved worldwide. www.zondervan.com

Scripture quotations marked NLT are taken from the *Holy Bible*, New Living Translation, copyright © 1996, 2004, 2015. Used by permission of Tyndale House Publishers, Inc., Carol Stream, Illinois 60188. All rights reserved.

Scripture marked NKJV taken from the New King James Version®. Copyright © 1982 by Thomas Nelson. Used by permission. All rights reserved.

The Christian Standard Bible. Copyright © 2017 by Holman Bible Publishers. Used by permission. Christian Standard Bible®, and CSB® are federally registered trademarks of Holman Bible Publishers, all rights reserved.

Scripture quotations marked ESV are from the ESV® Bible (The Holy Bible, English Standard Version®), copyright © 2001 by Crossway, a publishing ministry of Good News Publishers. Used by permission. All rights reserved. The Holy Bible, English Standard Version (ESV) is adapted from the Revised Standard Version of the Bible, copyright Division of Christian Education of the National Council of the Churches of Christ in the U.S.A. All rights reserved.

Published in the United States of America

10 9 8 7 6 5 4 3 2 1

ISBN-13: 978-1-952833-74-8
ISBN-10: 1-952833-74-4

Cover design by TJS Publishing House
Published by TJS Publishing House
www.tjspublishinghouse.com

CONTENTS

INTRODUCTION

At the age of 36, my life changed dramatically, but for the best. I spent so many years in the dark until I opened the Word and allowed it to truly be a lamp to my feet and a light to my path (Psalm 119:105 NIV). This journey taught me the importance of a real relationship with Jesus and how to love myself and others. It taught me how to forgive, even when I was still in pain, trust in uncertainty, and find hope when everything felt hopeless.

When I was given the prophecy that I had a book in me, the Lord gave me the title "Chapter 36." Not knowing how this would happen, I sat with the Lord, and as I spent time with Him, He gave me instructions. He wanted me to share pieces of my journey and how, at 36, my life changed dramatically, but for the best.

As you read this, I pray that you come to know the Jesus I know. I pray that He gives you ears to hear and eyes to see him in the small details others often miss. I pray that you read, reflect, and truly listen to what our Father is saying to you. I hope this helps you to understand that He speaks to us in unique ways. I pray that He changes your life dramatically for the best. Find your secret place and allow the Lord to speak to you through His Word or any way He chooses; we only need to listen and obey.

HOW TO USE THIS BOOK

This book is just one part of your journey with Jesus. To be most effective, it should be read daily. Over the next 36 days, I hope my walk with the Lord encourages you to sit with the Holy Spirit and really listen to what God wants to say. Each day will begin with a story of a personal struggle that the Lord has helped me overcome, and I pray it will help you see how He moves in your own life. Then, reflect by sitting with the Holy Spirit, reviewing the questions He has placed on my heart to share with you. After that, listen to what the Holy Spirit reveals, even if the answers are challenging.

I want you to know that this journey may not always be easy, but it is worth it. Know that each day, you are being healed and made whole in the Lord! Finally, conclude each day with prayer, allowing it to bring you closer to Jesus and strengthen your prayer life. I am excited to embark on this 36-day journey with you!

SCRIPTURE: I've included a scripture with each day's reading, but if the Lord leads you to another verse, feel free to use that and let Him speak to you! At the end of each section, take a moment to write down the scripture and reflect on each word.

REFLECT: Take a moment to reflect on the questions, allowing yourself to be still and listen for the Holy Spirit's guidance. Think about what the verse means to you. Do you feel the Lord is speaking to you about something specific? This is a personal journey, so take your time and really engage with each thought.

LISTEN: Take a moment to listen attentively to what the Holy Spirit may reveal to you. Listening involves being fully present and open, ready to absorb what God wants to communicate. As you quiet your mind, pay attention to any thoughts, feelings, or impressions that may come.

PRAY: Now pray, inviting God into your thoughts and feelings. Share with Him what's on your mind and ask for clarity and understanding regarding the scripture. This is your personal time to connect deeply with God, so be honest and open.

DAY 1

GET OUT OF YOUR OWN WAY

Ephesians 4:22-24 NIV

Enough was enough! I had been living an unfulfilling life, and it showed. The pain seeped out slowly every day through my words and actions; it was visible on my face, pure depression. Negative thoughts consumed my mind like a crowded hallway. I didn't know how to make them stop

I was tired of faking it, trying to hide my hurt with social drinking and fleeting happiness, living "the life" while feeling trapped in bondage. I wanted to be free. I felt like a prisoner in my relationship, I was tired of my job, and my mind was a mess. I knew there was something better out there for me, but I was too scared and complacent to go after it. I let the "good" life blind me.

They say wisdom comes with age, which can be true, but I believe that true wisdom comes from knowing and following Jesus Christ (Proverbs 2:6 NIV).

I had to get out of my own way and seek the Lord. He is the only one who can bring us out of the darkness. To get our attention, He allows us to fall to our knees, then begins to build us up again. That's exactly what happened to me. When depression set in, I had to fight. I ran straight to the Father. Don't give up and let the enemy win; keep fighting because victory is found in Him.

I began attending church, praying, reading the Word, and trying my best to stay in the presence of the Lord. I was seeking Him with my whole heart (Deuteronomy 4:29 NIV). I had to surrender! Don't get me wrong; it's not easy, and no one is perfect; we all fall short of the glory of God. The key is to get up with an understanding that the Lord has plans to give you a hope and a future (Jeremiah 29:11 NIV). If that's not a win, I don't know what is.

LET'S REFLECT

As you sit with the Holy Spirit, take a moment to reflect on these questions: Is there anything preventing you from walking in the freedom of the Lord? What plans are you trying to hold on to that you know aren't working?

LET'S LISTEN

Take a moment with the scripture below to reflect and listen, inviting the Holy Spirit to guide you in your current situation. Come with an open heart and expect the unexpected.

You were taught, with regard to your former way of life, to put off your old self, which is being corrupted by its deceitful desires; to be made new in the attitude of your minds; and put on the new self, created to be like God in true righteousness and holiness.

Ephesians 4:22-24 NIV

SCRIPTURE:

REFLECT:

LISTEN:

LET'S PRAY

Thank God for making you new in Christ. Ask Him to help you let go of old ways and embrace the transformation He's calling you to, living with a heart that reflects His truth and righteousness.

DAY 2
CLOSE TO THE BROKENHEARTED

Psalm 34:18 NIV

The Lord knows exactly what will get your attention to bring you back to Him. That very thing is usually whatever you have been putting before Him. For the Lord is a jealous God, and we are not to worship any other gods (Exodus 34:14 NIV). In my case, it was always a relationship. Without realizing it, I idolized them, putting their status and another person above myself.

The Lord made me a beautiful person. One who is very kind, loving, and serving, but in the past was very naive to foolishness. I walked in darkness, trying to fill a void only the Lord could fill in one failed relationship after another. Blessed are we that our Father will leave the 99 for the ONE (Matthew 18:10-14 NIV), and we are ALL the one.

With every failed relationship, my thoughts were to just get into another one. No big deal, but this time, the Lord had other plans. This one hit different; it knocked the breath out of me. I was crushed. This relationship left me feeling hopeless, confused, and on a path to self-destruction. I had no choice but to seek God. Seeking God taught me not only how to love myself the way He loves me, but others as well. Most importantly, I was taught not to accept anything less. We are to seek first His kingdom and righteousness, and everything else will be added to us (Matthew 6:33 NIV). When we sit in His presence and read the Word, it becomes a lamp to our feet and a light to our path (Psalm 119:105 NIV).

Jesus taught me my worth and showed me my true identity in Him. This process is not easy, and it does not happen overnight, but it's worth it. It's a lifestyle, a daily decision to die to your flesh. The Lord told us to delight ourselves in Him, and He will give us the desires of our hearts (Psalm 37:4 NIV). This pressing produced good fruit (Galatians 5:22-23 NIV) in me, discernment, alignment, light, and most importantly, a real relationship with Jesus.

LET'S REFLECT

As you sit with the Holy Spirit, take a moment to reflect on these questions: Have you been worshiping any idols? What voids are you trying to fill without the Lord? Are you holding on to anything or anyone that the Lord wants you to let go of?

LET'S LISTEN

Take a moment with the scripture below to reflect and listen, inviting the Holy Spirit to guide you in your current situation. Come with an open heart and expect the unexpected.

The Lord is close to the brokenhearted and saves those who are crushed in spirit.

Psalm 34:18 NIV

SCRIPTURE:

REFLECT:

LISTEN:

LET'S PRAY

Thank God for being near to the brokenhearted. Ask Him to comfort you in your pain and remind you of His presence, peace, and healing.

DAY 3
OVERCOMING SIN

1 Corinthians 6:18 NIV

Having sex was something that I never thought I had to give up. I felt that as long as I was doing it in a committed relationship, I was good. Can you see the way the enemy tries to flip the script? A sin is a sin, no matter how you try to justify it. The devil has been playing these same lame mind games since the beginning of time. When are we going to wake up and decide to resist?

I can recall a time, in the beginning of my walk with the Lord, when I was seeing this guy. This man was attractive on so many levels. I'm not gonna front, I wanted him. So one day, he invited me over to his house to hang out. As the day ended, I decided to stay the night. Yes, I know, it was a bad move. But given where I thought I was spiritually, I thought I would be able to resist. So, while we were in bed watching a movie, just chilling. If you know, you know. It starts with a hand on a thigh, or a back rub, and the rest is history.

Lord, help me was all I thought. My flesh and spirit were fighting! As he placed his hand on my thigh, I moved it. The struggle was real! The word says that we are to run from temptation and resist the devil, and he will flee (James 4:7 NIV). I kid you not; I had to get out of bed, go downstairs, get on my knees, and pray! There is power in prayer, and the Lord hears our cry for help. The Lord will give us a way out (1 Corinthians 10:13 NIV) when we call to him, and that's exactly what I had to do.

After my prayer, I went back upstairs to find that he had fallen asleep in that short time. Not a deep sleep, but enough to stop trying. I also went to sleep and never spent the night again. I had to learn the hard way, but I thank the Lord for being my strength in my time of weakness. This man was a gentleman, but still a man. Thankfully, he never forced himself on me. It was never him I was worried about.

Overcoming sexual sin is a process and one that needs to be surrendered fully to the Lord daily. Your sin may not be sexual, and that's great! But whatever it is, the same truth applies. I made a promise to the Lord and myself that I would not have sex outside of marriage again, and I can say with the help of the Lord, it has been 3 years now. By spending time with Jesus, He helped me to realize that my body is a temple and that I am to honor God with it (1 Corinthians 6:19 NIV).

LET'S REFLECT

As you sit with the Holy Spirit, take a moment to reflect on these questions: Are you justifying any sin in your life? Are you honoring God with your body? Is the Lord offering you a way out of sin that you are choosing to ignore?

LET'S LISTEN

Take a moment with the scripture below to reflect and listen, inviting the Holy Spirit to guide you in your current situation. Come with an open heart and expect the unexpected.

Flee from sexual immorality. All other sins a person commits are outside the body, but whoever sins sexually, sins against their own body.

1 Corinthians 6:18 NIV

SCRIPTURE:

REFLECT:

LISTEN:

LET'S PRAY

Thank God for giving you the strength to honor Him with your body. Ask Him to help you flee from anything that doesn't align with His will and to guide you in living a life of purity.

DAY 4

SHIFTING GEARS

Proverbs 3:5 NIV

I have always been someone who loves to take risks and try new things. I was a tomboy who would jump off rooftops as a child. If it was fun and a challenge, I was in! New things never scared me; they excited me. But, for some reason, this situation was different. In the winter of 2020, a tree fell on my car, and I was faced with the new challenge of buying another one.

You're probably thinking that buying a car is not scary, and you're right; that wasn't the scary part. What I noticed as I began to look for my next vehicle was that I had a strong desire to buy a manual car. I never wanted a stick, nor did I know how to drive one. After some time, I finally found one I liked but couldn't drive my car off the lot. Ha! God has a sense of humor. In the process of buying a car, I didn't realize how the Lord was setting me up for my next. I was hearing the word of God and obeying it, not knowing the blessing that would come from it (Luke 11:28 NIV).

The scary part came when it was time to drive that car in Atlanta traffic! If you have never driven a stick, getting out of 1st gear was the worst. If you don't balance the clutch and gas, the car will stall, it'll roll back on hills, and on top of all that, trying to merge into Atlanta traffic was a mess! But as we know, God doesn't give us a spirit of fear (2 Timothy 1:7 NIV), and I had to remind myself of this every time I got in the car. I didn't want to drive this car that I had such a strong desire to buy. I was scared, but through consistent prayer and trust in the Lord, I drove that car. It cut off on me, and I started it up again and kept on going. I overcame this fear with prayer every time I got behind the wheel (Psalm 34:4 NIV). This is where my journey of trust began and where my relationship with Jesus was born.

Driving a manual car has become second nature to me now— something I do without much thought, thanks to Jesus! This act of obedience has opened countless doors for me, some of which I may not even be aware of yet. This car has taken me places I never thought I'd go and has sparked conversations that have led me to meet some incredible people.

LET'S REFLECT

As you sit with the Holy Spirit, take a moment to reflect on these questions: What is fear holding you back from? Are you being obedient to the nudging of the Holy Spirit? Where do you need to let the Lord increase your trust in Him?

LET'S LISTEN

Take a moment with the scripture below to reflect and listen, inviting the Holy Spirit to guide you in your current situation. Come with an open heart and expect the unexpected.

Trust in the Lord with all your heart,
and lean not on your own understanding.

Proverbs 3:5 NIV

SCRIPTURE:

REFLECT:

LISTEN:

LET'S PRAY

Thank God for His faithfulness. Ask Him to help you trust Him completely, even when things don't make sense, and to guide you with His wisdom.

DAY 5

FOR THE LOVE OF MONEY

Matthew 6:24 NIV

Money is a necessity for all of us, but how do you really perceive it? Do you see it as a god or as a gift from God, a tool for advancing the kingdom, or simply for personal gain? Honestly, changing my perspective on money was challenging. The scripture tells us that the love of money is the root of all kinds of evil (1 Timothy 6:10 NIV). I never thought of it that way; I just knew that when I didn't have it, I craved it, and when I did have it, I clung to it tightly. I wasn't giving my 10 percent at all.

Reflecting on my journey, I realize I was idolizing money, treating it like a god without even recognizing it. I was trapped in a poverty mindset, letting the enemy convince me that I would never have enough. To break free from this way of thinking, I needed to spend time with the Lord, allowing Him to transform and renew my mind (Romans 12:2 NIV). Yet, that was just the start; the journey was only beginning.

My transformation wasn't instant. I earnestly began seeking the Lord in April of 2022 and felt convicted to begin tithing.

For the first time, I gave my ten percent, and I've remained faithful ever since. The Lord invites us to test Him in this, promising to open the windows of heaven and pour out blessings too great to contain (Malachi 3:10 NIV). He is not a man who can lie (Numbers 23:19 NIV). As I continue on this journey, the freedom from money that the Lord has granted me is a true blessing. I know without a doubt that He is my provider, and He has promised to meet all my needs (Philippians 4:19 NIV). While I trust Him wholeheartedly, I'm not perfect; I have to actively dismiss thoughts that don't align with God's Word every day.

The Lord will use your struggles as a pathway to freedom. I prayed for greater trust in Him regarding finances, and He guided me to leave a well-paying job for one that involved more than a 50% pay cut. As I lay in bed questioning this decision, He slapped me with the scripture, "You can't serve two masters" (Matthew 6:24 NIV). Now, in this situation, He is teaching me to place my trust in Him alone rather than relying on what's in my bank account.

LET'S REFLECT

As you sit with the Holy Spirit, take a moment to reflect on these questions: How do you perceive money in your life? Are you genuinely a cheerful giver? Do you rely on your own abilities for provision rather than trusting in God? If you're not tithing, what fears or obstacles are keeping you from taking that step?

LET'S LISTEN

Take a moment with the scripture below to reflect and listen, inviting the Holy Spirit to guide you in your current situation. Come with an open heart and expect the unexpected.

No one can serve two masters. Either you will hate the one and love the other, or you will be devoted to the one and despise the other. You cannot serve both God and money.

Matthew 6:24 NIV

SCRIPTURE:

REFLECT:

LISTEN:

LET'S PRAY

Thank God for being the true priority in your life. Ask Him to help you fully surrender your heart, choosing Him above all else, and freeing you from anything that competes for His place.

DAY 6

FULL CIRCLE MOMENT

Isaiah 60:22 NIV

Back in 2010, I was living in Michigan and had a strong passion for becoming an elementary teacher. I was in school, shadowing teachers, and getting the work done! I was convinced that I would finish my program, land a job, and everything would fall into place. But for some reason, I put it all down and walked away.

As life went on, I learned that while we make plans, the Lord directs our steps (Proverbs 16:9 NIV). After earning several credits, I decided to move to Atlanta, confident that my credits would transfer smoothly. However, once I arrived, everything fell apart. I had to find a job and a new place to live, and none of my credits transferred.

At the time, I was frustrated, but life moved on. I found a good-paying job and slowly let go of my dream of teaching. In my 20s in Atlanta, I was in the streets—not doing anything terrible, but I wasn't focused on God's Word. I believe that while God doesn't cause bad things to happen,

He allows them and uses them for our good (Romans 8:28 NIV). It was time for Him to sit me down.

I had been living life my way and thought nothing of it until I was involved in a single-car accident. Surviving it made me question why I was even here. Looking back, I know God was watching over me and protected me for a purpose (Psalm 138:7 NIV).

Something had to change. I knew God had a bigger purpose for my life. I went back to school and became a therapist in 2018, thinking I'd help children in a deeper way than just teaching. Over time, I felt God calling me to a sabbatical. As I obeyed and took a break from therapy, God opened the door for me to teach.

In just one week, I'll be closing out the school year as a 1st grade teacher! Nothing is impossible with God (Luke 1:37 NIV). In life, we often try to make things happen and get frustrated when they don't, without realizing it might not be the right time. This full-circle moment brought me to tears, reminding me that even when we forget our desires, God doesn't, and He'll bring them back when we least expect it.

LET'S REFLECT

As you sit with the Holy Spirit, take a moment to reflect on these questions: Are you trying to move ahead of God's perfect timing? Do your desires align with His? What is God telling you to focus on in this season?

LET'S LISTEN

Take a moment with the scripture below to reflect and listen, inviting the Holy Spirit to guide you in your current situation. Come with an open heart and expect the unexpected.

At the right time, I, the LORD, will make it happen.

Isaiah 60:22 NIV

SCRIPTURE:

REFLECT:

LISTEN:

LET'S PRAY

Thank God for His perfect timing and promises. Ask Him to help you trust that He will bring the right things in your life at the right moment, and that His plans for you are always for good.

DAY 7
OUTWARD APPEARANCES

1 Samuel 16:7 NIV

I want to share an unexpected encounter I had with the Lord, one that took me by surprise. It started like any other day. I woke up, prayed, got dressed, and headed out for work. On the way, I decided to make a quick stop at Dunkin' for an iced coffee. I placed my order and pulled off.

I got to work and I looked at the order written on the cup. Instantly, I was irritated. The cream-to-sugar ratio was all wrong, and I just knew it would be nasty! As soon as I thought this, the Lord interrupted my thoughts with a word. It was more of a warning. "Stop looking at outward appearances". It hit me so hard that I just stared at the cup, trying to process what I just heard.

I felt led to take a sip, even though the old me would have just thrown it away. When I tell you it was the best coffee they'd ever made for me! I was blown away! So many times, we as people judge things and people by how they look, that we miss the goodness on the inside. We get so wrapped up in our thoughts that we forget the Lord's thoughts are not our thoughts (Isaiah 55:8 NIV), and He knows what's at the core of everything.

Fast forward a year, and I'm at Dunkin' again. I ordered my coffee, pulled off, and took a sip. It was on point! I looked at the order on the cup and smiled. They had written the wrong order again! But this time, I smiled because the Holy Spirit brought this encounter back to me. Only this time, I passed the test.

LET'S REFLECT

As you sit with the Holy Spirit, take a moment to reflect on these questions: Are you judging anyone or anything by its outward appearance? If so, what is it? Ask the Holy Spirit to help you see things from the Lord's perspective.

LET'S LISTEN

Take a moment with the scripture below to reflect and listen, inviting the Holy Spirit to guide you in your current situation. Come with an open heart and expect the unexpected.

But the Lord said to Samuel, "Do not consider his appearance or his height, for I have rejected him. The Lord does not look at the things people look at. People look at the outward appearance, but the Lord looks at the heart."

1 Samuel 16:7 NIV

SCRIPTURE:

REFLECT:

LISTEN:

LET'S PRAY

Thank God for looking at your heart, not just your outward appearance. Ask Him to help you focus on what truly matters—your character and relationship with Him.

DAY 8

NEW BEGINNINGS

Philippians 4:19 NIV

I was full of fear and confusion, neither of which is from God. I was being kicked out of my home, not because of unpaid rent, but because of a failed relationship. I had nowhere to go, and this person didn't care. He angrily tossed my bags down the stairs. At the time, I was still caught up in situations I had no business being in, but looking back, I see that God was using this as the wake-up call I needed. It was His way of showing me that it was time to move forward, and this was the only way He could get my attention.

I packed up all my things, put them in storage, and went to visit my sister in Florida. During that time, I cleared my mind, reconnected with family, and spent time with Jesus. It never crossed my mind that I'd be homeless when I returned "home". As I reflect on this, I'm reminded of the story of Joseph. No matter how many things went wrong in his life, the Lord was always with him (Genesis 39:21 NIV). Looking back, I can see that God was with me, too. Even though I was in my pit moment, the palace was just on the other side.

Back in Atlanta, the Lord supernaturally provided me with a new job I didn't even apply for, paying more than I'd ever made. Praise God! For the next two months, I worked and stayed in a different Airbnb each week. I prayed continually (1 Thessalonians 5:17 NIV) for God to open the door to a home.

Led by the Holy Spirit, I started looking at apartments. I considered having a roommate to save money, but soon realized the Lord had something specific in mind for me. He wanted me to live alone, in a particular place. Over the months of being "homeless", I toured three apartments, but it wasn't until the third one that I felt something was different.

I toured the place and loved it, but I had a second appointment that day. I had to leave the first appointment to make it to the second on time. I arrived at the second complex, only to find the office closed. If this was not a sign from God, I don't know what is. Sitting in my car, frustrated after battling traffic to get there, the first apartment suddenly came to mind. Initially, I talked myself out of it because of the traffic, but I went as I was led. When I got there, I was greeted immediately and offered the application.

As I sat in the business center ready to submit my application, I paused and silently asked the Lord, "Is this it?" In that moment, my eyes were drawn to the street sign: Faith Ave. I felt a wave of peace and confirmation (Philippians 4:7 NIV) and hit submit. The next day, I was approved and moved in.

Sitting in my new place with just an air mattress, the peace of the Lord filled me. No more arguments or negativity. It was a breath of fresh air. I promised God I'd never live with another man outside of my husband, and I've kept that promise. All glory to Him. I love the area, and as I settled in, God reminded me of something I'd said years ago while driving home from grocery shopping: how I'd love to live here. I never knew I'd need to, but He did. It was all part of His plan (Romans 8:28 NIV).

LET'S REFLECT

As you sit with the Holy Spirit, take a moment to reflect on these questions: Are you staying still when God is calling you to move? Are you letting God transform you, even in fear?

LET'S LISTEN

Take a moment with the scripture below to reflect and listen, inviting the Holy Spirit to guide you in your current situation. Come with an open heart and expect the unexpected.

And my God will meet all your needs according to the riches of his glory in Christ Jesus.

Philippians 4:19 NIV

SCRIPTURE:

REFLECT:

LISTEN:

LET'S PRAY

Thank God for His provision. Ask Him to help you trust that He will meet all your needs, according to His riches and glory.

DAY 9
RECESS

Lamentations 3:23a NLT

Recess is the highlight of a first-grade child's day, a chance to run wild and scream without a care! You'd think they'd do anything to keep it, right? Not my class!

"RECESS" was boldly written on the board for everyone to see. Whenever the class got too loud or ignored instructions, a letter was taken away. Each letter resulted in a two-minute timeout. With recess only lasting 30 minutes, they could lose up to 10 minutes of playtime for poor choices. On some days, lost letters even carried over to the next day if they occurred after recess ended.

One morning, as my class sat on the carpet ready to begin, I stood behind them, distracted, staring at the "RECESS" letters on the board. They had already lost two letters the day before, and as I stared at them now, I felt the Lord speak to my heart.

While standing there, the Lord whispered a powerful message to my spirit about His grace and mercy. My first-grade students knew about God, and when He prompted me,

I spoke what He laid on my heart. I loved these teaching moments! I'm thankful to God for giving me the ability to speak His truth to children in a way they could understand. Once He finished speaking, I followed His lead and did exactly as He instructed.

As I stood in front of my class, I pointed to the recess letters they had lost the day before. I asked, "Do you think it's fair to be punished for something you did yesterday?" Then, I explained that God's mercy is new every morning and that He forgives us for the mistakes we've made in the past. I explained that just like God shows us grace, we should show grace to one another. It was a powerful moment, and after speaking, I replaced the two missing letters. But deep down, I knew this was about more than just recess; God was speaking to their hearts. He wanted them to understand His grace and mercy in their lives.

LET'S REFLECT

As you sit with the Holy Spirit, take a moment to reflect on these questions: Are you letting yesterday's mistakes define today, despite the grace of God? Have you truly accepted the forgiveness that's already been given?

LET'S LISTEN

Take a moment with the scripture below to reflect and listen, inviting the Holy Spirit to guide you in your current situation. Come with an open heart and expect the unexpected.

Great is his faithfulness; his mercies
begin afresh each morning.

Lamentations 3:23 NLT

SCRIPTURE:

REFLECT:

LISTEN:

LET'S PRAY

Thank God for His unfailing love and faithfulness. Ask Him to remind you daily of His mercies, which are new every morning.

DAY 10
DON'T DELAY

Isaiah 55:8 NIV

For the past two years, I kept hearing the name of a particular state. I would get visions, overhear random conversations, and see license plates everywhere! At first, I didn't understand why. I have no intention of moving. But over time, I felt a deep knowing in my spirit that God had an assignment for me there, and one day, I would move.

All I was given was the name of the state. But, just as scripture says, we prophecy in part (1 Corinthians 13:9 NIV), and that's all I had; part of the picture. I didn't know when or why, just that I was supposed to go. It was frustrating, and there were moments I wondered if I was hearing God right. But honestly, I knew I was being led.

One morning, as I was lying in bed, I heard the Lord tell me to pack. My lease wasn't up for another seven months, and I had no idea exactly where I was going. Months passed, and with three months left on my lease, I felt the nudge again. This time, I went and bought moving boxes, knowing it was a clear sign from God that it was time to transition. I still didn't know exactly where I was going, but I began to pack and give things away as led by the Holy Spirit.

As I obeyed, the next step came. A job I had seen months earlier in that state popped back into my mind. I'd told God I'd apply if it was still available. It was still there! I applied, and within hours, they offered me an interview. Even better, I got the job in the interview. Now I knew where I was moving.

Just like before, the Lord made it clear where He wanted me to live. I visited the place, and in my spirit, I knew it was home. I even tried to check out other places, but for various reasons, I couldn't. That only confirmed what I knew in my spirit. I applied for the apartment, was approved, and just like that, everything fell into place.

The peace I felt throughout the process was nothing but God's hand at work. When I first received the word that I was moving, I was afraid. By the time the move actually happened, I was at peace. He gave me the vision, but only revealed the next step once I obeyed the first: pack.

LET'S REFLECT

As you sit with the Holy Spirit, take a moment to reflect on these questions: What is God asking you to do that you've been avoiding? Are your choices slowing down your progress? What could you change today to move forward?

LET'S LISTEN

Take a moment with the scripture below to reflect and listen, inviting the Holy Spirit to guide you in your current situation. Come with an open heart and expect the unexpected.

"For my thoughts are not your thoughts, neither are your ways my ways," declares the Lord.

Isaiah 55:8 NIV

SCRIPTURE:

REFLECT:

LISTEN:

LET'S PRAY

Thank God for His higher ways and thoughts. Ask Him to help you trust His plan, knowing His wisdom far surpasses our understanding.

DAY 11

THE LORD WILL PROVIDE

Genesis 22:14 ESV

Just reading the title should be enough to stir us, right? That's the kind of faith we should have in God. I'll admit, some days I've got it, other days I'm struggling, convincing myself by saying, "Lord, I got that mustard seed."

When God told me to move, I had two more paychecks total, followed by a two-month gap before my new job started. It was tight! I had to pay rent for both places, utilities, gas, and food; none of it added up. I had no idea how it was all going to come together. In the past, I would've tried to figure it out on my own. But this time, I prayed first, and for a while, I felt at peace. Then, as the money started running out, I had to do something.

I found an app where you can pick up as many shifts as you want and get paid within two business days after completing each shift. Sounds good, right? I knew I was qualified, I got my first job, worked, and got paid. I went into the app to get another job and was denied. I tried again. Denied! At first, I didn't know what was going on. It's not that I wasn't qualified, but the Lord wanted me to trust Him fully financially. I'd never had to do that before because I always had money in the bank.

This was hard. I had no choice but to rest, pray, and worship. That's all I could do to keep my mind from being attacked by the enemy. Weeks passed, and then the Lord opened the door for me to work a full week. But just as quickly, He closed it again. This time, I understood what was happening. I put my trust in Him and thanked Him for the rest I had received while the doors were closed. A deep peace washed over me, knowing that if He called me to leave my job and move, He would provide. Once my mindset shifted, God moved.

God sent the right people to help with the move and provide the money I needed. Checks came in the mail, and I sold things to cover the costs. God showed up in a BIG way! By the end, I had more than enough and moved with what fit in two cars. When I got to my new place, I furnished it all with what God provided, with money left over! God is good, and my faith is stronger than ever. Remember, if it's God's will, it's God's bill!

LET'S REFLECT

As you sit with the Holy Spirit, take a moment to reflect on these questions: Do you trust the Lord even when the path ahead is unclear? Are you willing to surrender your situation to Him, trusting it will lead to your growth and His glory?

LET'S LISTEN

Take a moment with the scripture below to reflect and listen, inviting the Holy Spirit to guide you in your current situation. Come with an open heart and expect the unexpected.

**So Abraham called the name of that place,
"The Lord will provide", as it is said to this day,
"On the mount of the Lord it shall be provided."**

Genesis 22:14 ESV

SCRIPTURE:

REFLECT:

LISTEN:

LET'S PRAY

Thank God for being your provider. Ask Him to help you trust in His provision, even when the way ahead feels uncertain.

DAY 12

HEART DESIRES

Psalm 37:4 ESV

When I first pursued a career in Occupational Therapy, I knew it was my calling. I wanted to work with kids. I didn't just want to teach them. I wanted to make a deeper impact. I wanted to help them thrive in the classroom and unlock their full potential.

As the years went by, working as a therapist, something inside me changed. I went from being passionate about my career to feeling bored and unfulfilled. I had that feeling you get when you know there has to be more. So, I took a step back and tried working in a rehab center, but it still didn't satisfy me. With this feeling inside of me, I sought the Lord for answers, and He began to reveal my true purpose.

He showed me that my passion for working with children was still there, but He was calling me to serve them in a different way. A year later, as I was standing in my bathroom, God spoke clearly and told me to go back to school. I wasn't excited. So many reasons to resist came to mind, but I chose to obey. Now, I'm about to graduate with a degree in Christian studies with an emphasis in youth ministry. Looking back, I realize that we are always exactly where God wants us to be, and He uses every experience, every detour, to get us in perfect alignment with His plan. That feeling of unfulfillment is often God's way of letting us know we've finished this season, and it's time to move forward. It's His gentle push, guiding us toward the next step in our purpose.

LET'S REFLECT

As you sit with the Holy Spirit, take a moment to reflect on these questions: Is your heart following God's will, or your own desires? Are you blocking your blessings by trusting your own understanding instead of His plan?

LET'S LISTEN

Take a moment with the scripture below to reflect and listen, inviting the Holy Spirit to guide you in your current situation. Come with an open heart and expect the unexpected.

Delight yourself in the LORD, and
he will give you the desires of your heart.

Psalm 37:4 ESV

SCRIPTURE:

REFLECT:

LISTEN:

LET'S PRAY

Thank God for the desires He places in your heart. Ask Him to help you delight in Him, trusting that He will fulfill His good plans for you.

DAY 13
SELF DESTRUCTION

Proverbs 14:12 NIV

Sometimes, we don't catch the warning signs until it's too late. Before leaving Atlanta, I wanted to get my nails done at my favorite spot, but something didn't sit right. I felt like God was telling me not to go, even though I had been there a hundred times before. After sitting with it for a minute, I went to the nail shop.

I walked into the shop and noticed two new techs, but I didn't think much of it until they were assigned to do my nails. I figured it was no big deal. At first, everything seemed ok, and I thought maybe I was overthinking. But as time went on, I realized the one doing my feet wasn't putting much effort into my pedicure, and the one doing my nails completely ruined their shape—they were left ugly and fragile!

I had them stop the service, and I left! Long story short, I was told not to go, but I ignored the warning, and as a result, all my nails broke off! It might seem small, but God cares about every detail of our lives (1 Peter 5:7 NIV) and wants to protect us from life's mishaps. I had to learn that even when

I thought it was no big deal, if God told me "No," I needed to listen! Every sin brings some form of death (Romans 6:23 NIV), and while God doesn't force us to obey, we have to trust that when He gives us direction, it's for our good. He's such a loving Father.

LET'S REFLECT

As you sit with the Holy Spirit, take a moment to reflect on these questions: What's driving your self-destructive behaviors? Can you identify the triggers behind your choices? How can you trust God's plan for you despite your struggles?

LET'S LISTEN

Take a moment with the scripture below to reflect and listen, inviting the Holy Spirit to guide you in your current situation. Come with an open heart and expect the unexpected.

"There is a way that appears to be right,
but in the end it leads to death."

Proverbs 14:12 NIV

SCRIPTURE:

REFLECT:

LISTEN:

LET'S PRAY

Thank God for guiding you in truth. Ask Him to help you trust His ways, knowing that His path leads to life, even when other options seem tempting.

DAY 14

PEOPLE PLEASER

Galatians 1:10 NIV

Being a people pleaser was something that I battled with for so long. I wanted to make everyone happy, not knowing that it was slowly sucking the life out of me. In the Word, it says that we are dead in our sins, that we don't know that we are walking in bondage until God wakes us up (Colossians 2:13 NIV).

I can reflect on a time when I'd had enough. I was overpleasing people in a way that caused me mental, physical, and emotional turmoil. I'd accepted a job that I would soon learn would be a drain on my spirit. Looking back, I can see its purpose, but walking it in was a struggle. Day after day was filled with uncertainty. People were calling off, showing up late, and so much more. Because I worked for the Lord, I was reliable and willing to help where needed, and they took advantage of this.

From my very first day and many months to follow, I was saying yes to something I really didn't want to do, until one day I said no. As you can imagine, this was a problem! People are happy when you are pleasing them, but quickly forget once you can't. That particular day, I was not feeling well and struggled to even come to work. I was capable of doing my job, and that was it! Of course, someone called off, and when asked if I could cover their job, I said no with a reason why and in a respectful manner.

Instantly, my supervisor was angry, forgetting all the times I offered or agreed to help. They never even asked how I was feeling, and then told me I had no choice. This is what being a people pleaser got me. So, at that moment, I gave them a choice: to stay and do my job or go home. Long story short, I walked out and went home, but at that very moment, the chains of being a people pleaser were broken off me.

I'm not saying I handled the situation 100% correctly, but I was free. God allowed that moment to help change my view of myself and the way others saw me. Shockingly, from that day on, I returned to work and was shown respect for standing up for myself and not being a pushover. Through it all, I maintained a humble attitude and let the Lord work through me, recognizing that this was about something much bigger than myself.

LET'S REFLECT

As you sit with the Holy Spirit, take a moment to reflect on these questions: Where are you seeking approval from others instead of God? What fears drive your need to please people? How can you refocus on God's guidance?

LET'S LISTEN

Take a moment with the scripture below to reflect and listen, inviting the Holy Spirit to guide you in your current situation. Come with an open heart and expect the unexpected.

"Am I now trying to win the approval of human beings, or of God? Or am I trying to please people? If I were still trying to please people, I would not be a servant of Christ."

Galatians 1:10 NIV

SCRIPTURE:

REFLECT:

LISTEN:

LET'S PRAY

Thank God for His approval over your life. Ask Him to help you seek His approval above all else, living to please Him rather than others.

DAY 15
RESTORATION

James 2:26 ESV

Family is everything, and there is nothing like getting together to reminisce and enjoy those inside jokes that only those closest to you get. But life happens, and people drift apart. In my case, I went through a season of isolation, sometimes going months without hearing from my family.

As I was in my bathroom one morning, the Holy Spirit spoke to me, prompting me to start a group text with all my siblings and cousins to catch up. I missed my family and wanted to hear from them, but someone had to take the first step. I got my phone, typed out a message, and hit send. As I sent it, I heard in my spirit, "Faith without works is dead." (James 2:26, ESV) I had all the hope and faith that we would reconnect, but if I didn't send the message, it would never happen. My plan was a monthly meet-up and a consistent group chat to stay in touch. I didn't let any negative thoughts flood my mind; I simply obeyed.

A little while later, everyone responded with love, sharing that they'd had the same thoughts I had, but no one reached out to initiate anything! I am so grateful that the Holy Spirit led me. He knew the right time and when every heart would be open to this, as we had times in the past when this would not have been a good idea. That's why it is so important to be led by the Holy Spirit in all things. God sees what's ahead when we can't, and He protects us along the way.

LET'S REFLECT

As you sit with the Holy Spirit, take a moment to reflect on these questions: How do you recognize the Holy Spirit's guidance in your daily life? How might being led by Him shape your choices and relationships? Can you recall a moment when you felt a strong sense of direction or conviction?

LET'S LISTEN

Take a moment with the scripture below to reflect and listen, inviting the Holy Spirit to guide you in your current situation. Come with an open heart and expect the unexpected.

"For as the body apart from the spirit is dead,
so also faith apart from works is dead."

James 2:26 ESV

SCRIPTURE:

REFLECT:

LISTEN:

LET'S PRAY

Thank God for the gift of faith. Ask Him to help you live out your faith through actions, showing His love in everything you do

DAY 16

PRAY

1 Thessalonians 5:17 ESV

Prayer is powerful, but it's easy to question its impact, especially when we're waiting for change. When I started my journey with the Lord, I accepted this. However, I still wondered if I would truly make a difference.

Yet, I kept praying for the people and situations in my life that I longed to see change. It was not easy, as I wanted to see them happen immediately. God had to teach me that things happen in His timing and not mine. I feel that He also used this to develop my patience. I have been praying for a close friend and family for about a year now, and for a long time, I saw nothing. I was frustrated at times because I felt my words were not heard.

I still continued to pray, believing that if I had faith the size of a mustard seed, God would move. As time passed, it felt like a sudden moment when God revealed what He had been orchestrating behind the scenes. He showed me that He had heard and was responding to every prayer I had spoken.

Members of my family were slowly coming to the Lord, doors were opening, and I was walking in the Lord's favor.

Witnessing the answers to my prayers has genuinely deepened my faith and trust in God. I am reminded that He is faithful, loving, and truly cares about everything that matters to us (1 Peter 5:7 ESV). As I write this, I realize He's revealing that my heart posture needed to shift for me to witness any change. I had the wrong intentions behind my prayers, sometimes seeking selfish gain. When we pray for others, it's essential to keep our focus genuinely on them.

So, let's pray, pray about that family member or friend the Lord has placed on your heart, asking Him to guide your intentions and align your heart with His.

LET'S REFLECT

As you sit with the Holy Spirit, take a moment to reflect on these questions: Are you entering into prayer with the right heart and intentions? Do you truly believe that your prayers will be answered? What steps can you take to deepen your faith in God's promises as you wait for those answers?

LET'S LISTEN

Take a moment with the scripture below to reflect and listen, inviting the Holy Spirit to guide you in your current situation. Come with an open heart and expect the unexpected.

pray without ceasing,

1 Thessalonians 5:17 ESV

SCRIPTURE:

REFLECT:

LISTEN:

LET'S PRAY

Thank God for always being near and available. Ask Him to help you pray without ceasing, keeping your heart connected to Him throughout your day.

DAY 17

10 PERCENT

Malachi 3:10 NIV

I remember sitting on my bed, watching a live sermon, and feeling inspired. When it was time to give, I took out my card and decided to give my full ten percent. Tithing was a big deal for me because I had never really tithed before, and if I did, it was never the whole amount.

I vividly remember the rush of emotion after I hit submit, and my payment was processed. In that moment, I felt a sense of freedom, as if chains were being broken. God invites us to test Him in this, and I didn't even realize that's exactly what I was doing! From that point on, I committed to giving ten percent every time I got paid. There were moments when it was a struggle, but I refused to let the enemy hold me back, no matter how hard he tried!

I would often find myself flooded with thoughts like, "You could save this," or "You could use it for something else," or "You don't have to give it all." But each time, I made an effort to push those thoughts aside and quickly hit submit. Once I completed the payment, those thoughts disappeared. It's important to recognize that the devil uses the same tactics he used with Eve in the garden.

These thoughts weren't harsh or aggressive; they simply made me question whether I truly heard the Lord. The Bible tells us to resist the devil, and he will flee (James 4:7 NIV). Knowing God's Word helps us stand firm when the enemy tries to lead us astray. In those moments, the Holy Spirit reminds us of the truth, allowing us to reject thoughts that don't align with God's teachings.

As time went on, I began to experience a whole new sense of freedom and a fresh perspective on money. I learned to trust the Lord as my provider instead of relying solely on my bank account. Even when fear crept in, I turned to prayer, reminding myself that God had me covered. There were moments when I tithed despite my account looking a bit empty, and somehow, He always made a way. I can't count how many times I needed money for something important and didn't have it, only to receive unexpected deposits, Apple Pay from loved ones, or checks in the mail just when I needed them!

He is an always-on-time God, and His promises are true. All you need to do is believe! If you're unsure about giving, take a leap of faith and trust in Him. I promise you, when you give, you'll receive back far more than you ever imagined in Jesus' name!

LET'S REFLECT

As you sit with the Holy Spirit, take a moment to reflect on these questions: In what ways have you experienced God's provision in your life, and how can those experiences encourage you to trust Him more with your money? How does your perspective on money change when you view it as a tool for God's purposes rather than just a personal resource?

LET'S LISTEN

Take a moment with the scripture below to reflect and listen, inviting the Holy Spirit to guide you in your current situation. Come with an open heart and expect the unexpected.

> **"Bring the whole tithe into the storehouse, that there may be food in my house. Test me in this," says the Lord Almighty, "and see if I will not throw open the floodgates of heaven and pour out so much blessing that there will not be room enough to store it."**
>
> **Malachi 3:10 NIV**

SCRIPTURE:

REFLECT:

LISTEN:

LET'S PRAY

Thank God for His promise to provide abundantly. Ask Him to help you trust in His provision and to give with a grateful and generous heart.

DAY 18

YOU KNOW MY VOICE

John 10:27 NIV

Throughout this journey, I've often found myself questioning whether what I heard was truly the voice of the Lord. Yet, time and again, people have affirmed (without me even asking) that I do know His voice. Now it's your turn to reflect on this. I'm here to tell you that you also recognize the voice of the Lord. When will you choose to believe that?

It's important to realize that truly knowing His voice doesn't happen overnight. For most of us, it unfolds gradually as we spend more time in His Word and in His presence. We often long for that dramatic burning-bush experience, hoping to hear a massive voice calling our name. But the truth is, that's not how it works for everyone. Instead, it's in the quiet moments and gentle whispers that we really begin to understand His guidance (1 Kings 19:12 NIV). This is how we truly understand how God speaks to us as individuals.

After my baptism in 2022, dreams and visions suddenly became a significant part of my life. Even though I had experienced encounters with the Lord before, I never realized it was Him speaking to me. While I still don't always grasp everything He's saying, I've learned that in time, things become clear.

I soon recognized that He was speaking to me in various ways, not just through dreams and visions, but also through songs, conversations with others, and reading the Bible. If we open our hearts, He can communicate with us in so many beautiful ways! There were times when I would see or hear a person's name, and soon after, they would reach out to me. He gifted me with numerous visions and dreams about things that were to come in my life. This preparation helped me stay ready and always remember to give Him the glory when those moments unfolded. God is incredibly patient and loves to confirm His word to us in countless ways because He genuinely wants to communicate with us.

What truly reassures me that I'm hearing my Father's voice is the deep sense of peace that comes with His message. God's voice will always align with what is written in His Word, so we have to turn to the Bible to confirm everything we hear and test the spirit (1 John 4:1 NIV). Remember, the Word of God doesn't bring confusion, anxiety, hopelessness, bitterness, or fear, but brings clarity, hope, joy, and confidence!

LET'S REFLECT

As you sit with the Holy Spirit, take a moment to reflect on these questions: How do you discern between your own thoughts and the voice of God, especially in moments of uncertainty or confusion? In what ways do you feel God has spoken to you personally, and how did those experiences impact your faith journey? When you hear God's voice, what emotions or thoughts accompany that message, and how do they align with Scripture?

LET'S LISTEN

Take a moment with the scripture below to reflect and listen, inviting the Holy Spirit to guide you in your current situation. Come with an open heart and expect the unexpected.

"My sheep hear my voice, and
I know them, and they follow me."

John 10:27 NIV

SCRIPTURE:

REFLECT:

LISTEN:

LET'S PRAY

Thank God for speaking to you. Ask Him to help you hear His voice clearly and follow His guidance with trust and obedience.

DAY 19

CHANGE YOUR PERSPECTIVE

Romans 12:2 NIV

I woke up this morning with a smile on my face as my alarm went off for work, something I've never experienced before! Just a week ago, I was grumbling about having to go to work. But as soon as those negative words left my lips, I paused and prayed to God, asking Him to help me change my attitude and to be grateful for the opportunity to work.

For much of my life, I was a chronic complainer, completely unaware that it was a problem until God opened my eyes. I would gripe about the simplest things; it felt like a natural response. I often found myself mean and angry when things didn't go my way, not realizing how this negativity made me unappealing inside and out. My attitude was just stank because of the words I allowed to slip from my mouth! When I discovered that "out of the abundance of the heart the mouth speaks" (*Matthew 12:34 NIV*), I was shocked to see how my words truly reflected the state of my heart.

I realized it was about more than just my words; it was a deeper issue rooted in my heart. Whenever we tackle surface problems, we often need to address deeper roots, and God wanted to help me with the source of my negativity. They say you become a product of your environment, and I grew up in a home filled with yelling and complaining. Naturally, I absorbed those negative behaviors, thinking that was how to get my way. It took some soul-searching to understand that I had to break that cycle and let God transform my heart so that my mind could be renewed.

Through consistent prayer and fasting, I began asking God to help me guard my mouth and take my thoughts captive. As I embraced this disciplined lifestyle, I noticed a transformation—not only in how I viewed complaints but also in how my grumbling shifted toward praise and gratitude. I'm not perfect, and there are still moments when a complaint might slip out. But thanks to God, I'm quicker to redirect those thoughts and express gratitude for the very things I used to complain about.

Walking with the Lord is a marathon, not a sprint. It's a daily journey we commit to until we're called home. God knows we can't do anything on our own; He is our ultimate source of strength. Let the Lord change your view of the world and the things around you. No matter what challenges you face, remember that after you've done all you can—through prayer, overcoming negative thoughts, and fasting—you can rest in the assurance that you are accepted by Jesus. He is always fighting for you.

LET'S REFLECT

As you sit with the Holy Spirit, take a moment to reflect on these questions: How does your perspective shape your experiences in the world? Have you asked God to reveal any issues in your heart? What steps can you take today to open your heart to God's transformative work?

LET'S LISTEN

Take a moment with the scripture below to reflect and listen, inviting the Holy Spirit to guide you in your current situation. Come with an open heart and expect the unexpected.

"Do not conform to the pattern of this world, but be transformed by the renewing of your mind. Then you will be able to test and approve what God's will is–his good, pleasing and perfect will."

Romans 12:2 NIV

SCRIPTURE:

REFLECT:

LISTEN:

LET'S PRAY

Thank God for renewing your mind. Ask Him to help you resist the patterns of this world and align your thoughts with His will, so you can live out His good purpose for your life.

DAY 20

DON'T GIVE UP ON GOD

Ephesians 3:20 ESV

Today's entry is a little different. As I sat here asking the Lord what to write about, I heard Him say, "Don't give up on God." He provided me with today's scripture and placed it on my heart that His children need encouragement. Just like everything I've shared in this book, this message is led by the Holy Spirit and today is no exception. Hopefully, by now you understand that obedience is better than sacrifice, and when the Lord tells me to do something, I follow through!

When the Lord placed it on my heart that I had a book inside me, I felt a rush of excitement. After a prophet confirmed this word, I knew I had to dive in, but I was completely unsure of where to begin. The whole process felt overwhelming. I didn't know what kind of book He wanted me to write until the title was finally revealed. One morning, I heard clearly, "Chapter 36," and I realized God wanted me to create a devotional, but with a unique twist. He urged me to share pieces of my personal journey. At first, the task felt daunting, and I often doubted myself—more importantly, I doubted the God within me.

I would write a bit, then stop, and this cycle went on for months. At one point, I even set the project aside entirely. But what I love about God is that He won't let you forget what He wants you to accomplish. He brings it back to your mind until you're ready to act. God understands the right timing for everything, and you can trust that His timing is always perfect.

One day, while scrolling through YouTube, I came across a sister in Christ hosting a 12-week class designed to help us stay consistent in pursuing what God has called us to do. After praying about it, I felt confirmed to join. In the class, we were asked to identify three goals we wanted to focus on. After praying, my book came to mind. I committed to writing one entry a week, and I've done my best to stay faithful ever since. What I quickly realized is that it was always about my relationship with Jesus. The closer I drew to the Lord, the easier it became to write, and eventually, I completed the book.

I also learned just how strategic God is—He truly has everything planned out. Once I committed to focusing on finishing my book, I unexpectedly ran into a friend I hadn't seen in over 10 years! It was no coincidence that she had written a book herself, and during our conversation, she shared her publisher's information with me. When I say the Lord is in every detail and goes before us, I mean it! Remember, if the Lord has called you to it, He will see you through it! Trust Him, because as Ephesians 3:20 ESV reminds us, He can do immeasurably more than we can ask or imagine!

LET'S REFLECT

As you sit with the Holy Spirit, take a moment to reflect on these questions: What specific calling or task has God placed on your heart during this season? How can you pray for God to reveal the helpers for your calling? Are there areas where you find yourself doubting that God can use you to fulfill the calling He has placed on your heart?

LET'S LISTEN

Take a moment with the scripture below to reflect and listen, inviting the Holy Spirit to guide you in your current situation. Come with an open heart and expect the unexpected.

"Now to him who is able to do far more abundantly than all that we ask or think, according to the power at work within us."

Ephesians 3:20 ESV

SCRIPTURE:

REFLECT:

LISTEN:

LET'S PRAY

Thank God for His ability to do immeasurably more than we ask or imagine. Ask Him to help you trust in His limitless power and believe that He can work beyond your expectations.

DAY 21

GOD IS LOVE

1 John 4:8 NIV

Even before I began my steady walk with the Lord, I often wrestled with the question: How can I love a God or anything I can't see? This struggle lasted for a long time, and I just couldn't find that connection. I didn't want to go through the motions without genuine emotion faking it until I made it. I yearned to truly feel His love.

I used to think that accepting Christ would instantly fill me with His love, but it never occurred to me that building that love was just like any other relationship. It takes time. Each day, I spent time with Jesus, reading His Word, talking to Him, and going to church on Sundays. Little did I know, He was slowly teaching me what love truly is: how to receive it, how to give it, and, most importantly, about Himself. Eventually, that question faded away as I began to truly experience His love in my life.

It was a challenging journey for me because I spent years believing I understood love, how to receive it and give it, without realizing I was approaching it from a worldly perspective. I had been programmed to love conditionally, which contradicted everything the Bible teaches about love. Scripture tells us that love is patient, kind, not proud, not self-seeking, not easily angered, and doesn't keep a record of wrongs (1 Corinthians 13:4-6 NIV). I felt deeply convicted by this passage, but I now knew exactly why I had trouble experiencing the true love of God.

The Lord had to strip away all my wrong teachings and rebuild me in His love, aligning me with how He originally created me to be. He did this through trials, using real-life experiences to help me bear the fruit of the Spirit (Galatians 5:22 NIV). Time and again, the Lord showed me that His love for me is unconditional and that I was called to extend that same love to others, even when they hurt me. He taught me that this didn't mean I had to keep those people in my life; I simply needed to live in a way that reflects His light in every area.

God taught me through His Word that He is love, and when we learn to love from the true source, our understanding of love transforms. We begin to operate from a cup that overflows, allowing us to love from a place of wholeness rather than emptiness. If you find yourself in this situation, I encourage you to open your Bible and spend time in the Word of God. Look up scriptures about love and allow the Lord to speak to your heart. Engaging in worship, connecting with fellow believers, or even serving others can help you profoundly experience the love of God. Remember, the more you seek Him, the more you'll discover the depth of His love for you, and it has the power to transform your life in ways you never imagined.

LET'S REFLECT

As you sit with the Holy Spirit, take a moment to reflect on these questions: Do you find it difficult to experience the love of God, and if so, what challenges do you face? How can you actively seek to experience God's love more? Are there beliefs that keep you from feeling loved by God?

LET'S LISTEN

Take a moment with the scripture below to reflect and listen, inviting the Holy Spirit to guide you in your current situation. Come with an open heart and expect the unexpected.

"Whoever does not love does not know God, because God is love."

1 John 4:8 NIV

SCRIPTURE:

REFLECT:

LISTEN:

LET'S PRAY

Thank God for His perfect love. Ask Him to help you understand and experience His love more deeply, so you can reflect it to others.

DAY 22

NO OTHER CHOICE

Joshua 24:15 NIV

As individuals, we inherently desire to serve something or someone, and we all recognize the existence of God. Whether you acknowledge it or not, you are either aligned with the kingdom of darkness or the kingdom of light. Many find themselves straddling both realms, but as Scripture warns, the Lord will spit those out who are lukewarm (Revelation 3:16 NIV).

Being lukewarm often reveals itself in subtle yet telling ways, reflecting a lack of genuine commitment. Picture someone who prays only in times of crisis, missing out on the transformative power of a consistent prayer life. They may worship selectively, joining in only when it's convenient, rather than engaging with a heartfelt desire to connect with God. Many allow the pressures of the world to shape their values, leading to compromised beliefs. Without community support and accountability, they often drift into isolation. This half-hearted approach creates a disconnect, leaving them caught between the kingdoms of light and darkness, longing for deeper meaning yet hesitant to fully commit.

I can definitely relate to this struggle and often found myself with one foot in each world. One of the hardest challenges for me has been staying consistent with reading my Bible. I'm sure many of you have experienced this: you sit down wide awake, ready to dive into the Word, and suddenly you start yawning. Before you know it, you've drifted off into one of the best naps you've had in a while! John 8:44 *NIV* reminds us that the devil is a liar and the father of lies, always trying to distract us from our true connection with God. In moments of worship when I felt completely disconnected, I would ask the Lord what was happening, and it became clear that my inconsistent prayer life and lack of time in the Word were the culprits. It's a powerful reminder that nurturing our prayer life and Scripture reading is essential for deepening our relationship with Him.

So how do we fix this? For me, it all started with praying and asking the Holy Spirit to help me stay consistent in my prayer life and Bible reading. Am I perfect? Definitely not, but I'm giving it my best shot, and over time, it has become easier. I also made it a point to thank God whenever I completed something I knew He had helped me with. Another step I took was joining a small group at my church for accountability and consistency. As James 4:8 NIV reminds us, when we draw near to God, He draws near to us.

The more I engaged in these practices, the more I found myself naturally speaking to God throughout the day, sharing my life with Him, and thanking Him for His protection and guidance. I realized that worship isn't about me; it's about glorifying God and declaring His holiness. I'd focused on the wrong things, and God shifted my perspective. Allow the Lord to transform you fully, and you'll discover that there truly is no other choice but to live for Him!

LET'S REFLECT

As you sit with the Holy Spirit, take a moment to reflect on these questions: What specific areas of your life are you holding back from fully committing to your faith, and how do those hesitations impact your relationship with God? In what ways can you actively cultivate a deeper connection with God that moves you from being lukewarm to passionate in your faith?

LET'S LISTEN

Take a moment with the scripture below to reflect and listen, inviting the Holy Spirit to guide you in your current situation. Come with an open heart and expect the unexpected.

"But if serving the Lord seems undesirable to you, then choose for yourselves this day whom you will serve, whether the gods your ancestors served beyond the Euphrates, or the gods of the Amorites, in whose land you are living. But as for me and my household, we will serve the Lord."

Joshua 24:15 NIV

SCRIPTURE:

REFLECT:

LISTEN:

LET'S PRAY

Thank God for the freedom to choose Him. Ask Him to help you wholeheartedly serve Him, no matter what others may choose.

DAY 23
FORGIVE YOURSELF

Hebrews 8:12 NIV

At 19, I was away at college, living my best life and finally in my first relationship. Back at home, I wasn't allowed to talk on the phone with boys, so dating one was out of the question. But here, things were different; I had more freedom. As the days passed, we got closer until we eventually took that next step in our relationship.

I can remember that night as if it were yesterday. After we finished, I was rushing off to work, sprinting across campus and nearly late for my shift in the cafeteria. Once I arrived, my mind was consumed with thoughts of what had just happened. It wasn't all butterflies; I was filled with mixed emotions—excitement and the thrill of being in love, but underneath it all, I felt a wave of shame for no longer being a virgin. With the pain and discomfort still fresh, I pushed through and tried to carry on with my day.

Before long, my appetite shifted, and I found myself constantly hungry! The thought of being pregnant didn't even cross my mind until one day when a friend pointed out that I was eating more than usual. She asked if I was pregnant, and I denied it—ain't no way, I thought! But the question stuck with me.

Not long after that, my boyfriend and I made a trip to Planned Parenthood, where we received the news that no 19-year-old wants to hear: I was pregnant. Overwhelmed with fear of what my mother would think and how this would change my life, I took a pill and terminated the pregnancy. In that moment, I felt relief, but little did I know that I wouldn't find peace for years to come. I confided in almost no one, feeling so ashamed and guilty that I tried to bury the experience deep down. I repented countless times, pleading with the Lord for forgiveness, yet I struggled to fully release it and forgive myself. Eventually, I realized that it wasn't God holding this against me; it was the devil, wanting me to walk in shame and hide from the Lord, just like Adam and Eve did in the garden (Genesis 3:8-10 NIV).

This sin kept me from God for so many years, as I felt unworthy and too ashamed to be used by Him. Eventually, I learned to come to God just as I am, seeking His healing and the renewal of my mind. Bringing my shame to Him was what truly healed me; it was a slow journey, but one that was absolutely worth it. Many people believe they need to clean themselves up before approaching God, but the truth is the opposite: we can't do this without Him! The Word tells us that anyone who is in Christ is a new creation; the old has gone, and the new is here (2 Corinthians 5:17 NIV).

The Lord reminds us that if we confess our sins, He is faithful and just to forgive us and purify us from all unrighteousness (1 John 1:9 NIV). We must believe in the truth of God's Word—He never contradicts Himself. Once I truly grasped the nature of God and His promises, I found freedom. God forgave me long ago, but I allowed the enemy to keep me in bondage. So take a moment to forgive yourself for whatever comes to mind as you read this and remember that God has already done so. He loves you and chooses not to remember your past sins. Once you repent, you are forgiven.

LET'S REFLECT

As you sit with the Holy Spirit, take a moment to reflect on these questions: What specific past mistakes or regrets are you holding onto that prevent you from fully embracing God's forgiveness and moving forward in your life? How can you begin to see yourself through God's eyes, recognizing that His grace has already covered your sins and that you are worthy of forgiveness and healing?

LET'S LISTEN

Take a moment with the scripture below to reflect and listen, inviting the Holy Spirit to guide you in your current situation. Come with an open heart and expect the unexpected.

"For I will forgive their wickedness
and will remember their sins no more."

Hebrews 8:12 NIV

SCRIPTURE:

REFLECT:

LISTEN:

LET'S PRAY

Thank God for His mercy and forgiveness. Ask Him to help you fully embrace His grace, knowing that He remembers your sins no more.

DAY 24
ROOTED IN CHRIST

Galatians 2:20 NIV

I can't quite remember when it all started, but for years, I was completely absorbed in my daily horoscope, eagerly reading each prediction tied to my zodiac sign. I invested so much hope in those readings, believing they held the keys to my future and my happiness. It felt so real, and with my spiritual eyes closed, I didn't see the danger lurking beneath the surface. I was unknowingly falling prey to the enemy's schemes, keeping me trapped in darkness. Looking back now, it's clear that those messages were a distraction, masking the truth I desperately needed to see—the truth of who I am in Christ, a truth that brings light and purpose to my life.

But that's the plan of the devil, right? To keep us spiritually blinded so that we continue to unknowingly build his kingdom. If he attacked Jesus' identity in Matthew chapter 4, what makes you think he won't attack ours? I always say that satan comes as close to the light as he can get (2 Corinthians 11:14 NIV). The enemy knows that when we don't know who we are, he can deceive us, distract us, and condemn us, and that is exactly what zodiac signs do. They are sprinkled with just enough truth that we don't investigate them further; instead, we come into agreement with them and the father of lies.

Zodiac signs are a clever tactic of satan to confuse God's people about their true identity, sowing doubt and confusion that ultimately can lead you away from His perfect will. The enemy is out to steal, kill, and destroy (John 10:10 NIV), and it's time to wake up! We need to see these traps for what they are and boldly stand in the truth of our identity in Christ, refusing to be swayed by the lies.

But how do we make this happen? We dive into the Word, allowing it to be our lamp and light (Psalm 119:105 NIV). Here's the truth: darkness has to flee when the light breaks through, so let God's Word illuminate your path. Pray for discernment, because we often get tangled in overthinking when the answers are right in front of us. Ask the Lord to reveal His truth, and trust that He will come through for you. Remember, the Word says we have not because we have not asked (James 4:2 NIV), so don't hesitate; approach His throne with confidence.

Embrace the guidance of the Holy Spirit, who is eager to lead you into all truth and help you discern what's right. It's time to break free from the chains of doubt and confusion. Stand firm in your identity, knowing you are a masterpiece designed for greatness. Step into your calling with courage and let His light shine through you. The world is waiting for you to fulfill your purpose; don't keep it waiting any longer!

LET'S REFLECT

As you sit with the Holy Spirit, take a moment to reflect on these questions: What lies or negative thoughts do you struggle with that make you doubt your identity in Christ? In which areas do you often question your identity in Christ, and what actions can you take to overcome that doubt and embrace who you truly are?

LET'S LISTEN

Take a moment with the scripture below to reflect and listen, inviting the Holy Spirit to guide you in your current situation. Come with an open heart and expect the unexpected.

"I have been crucified with Christ, and I no longer live, but Christ lives in me. The life I now live in the body, I live by faith in the Son of God, who loved me and gave himself for me."

Galatians 2:20 NIV

SCRIPTURE:

REFLECT:

LISTEN:

LET'S PRAY

Thank God for sending Jesus to give you new life. Ask Him to help you live each day fully surrendered to Him, letting His love and power shape who you are.

DAY 25

TRUSTING GOD'S PROMISES

Luke 1:37 NIV

If you're waiting on a promise from God, you know the waiting game can be a real struggle. It's all too easy to feel discouraged or even lost, especially when the blessing feels far away. When God first gave me a promise of marriage, I was filled with excitement, expecting it to happen quickly. But I quickly learned that the promise wasn't just around the corner. There was a lot the Lord needed to refine and strip away in me first, preparing me to truly embrace and steward that blessing when it finally came.

At first, the hardest struggle for me was the waiting. It was so challenging that I found myself replaying the promise in my mind, constantly doubting whether I had truly heard God right. I became so fixated on the promise itself that I lost sight of the One who made it. In those moments, I realized that I was prioritizing the promise over my relationship with God. We are called to walk by faith, not by sight (2 Corinthians 5:7 NIV), and this truth hit me hard. Just like Peter walking on water—when he took his eyes off Jesus, he sank! His experience serves as a powerful reminder that our focus should always be on God, not on the gifts He gives us. We must ensure that nothing (not even God's promises) takes precedence over our relationship with Him, because it is through that relationship that we find true peace and guidance during our waiting seasons.

During this long process, I came to realize that I had started to idolize the promise itself, losing sight of God's warning against idolatry. In Deuteronomy 5:7-9 NIV, He reminds us not to have any other gods before Him because He is a jealous God. Focusing too much on the promise only led to hurt, disappointment, confusion, and anxiety. But I began to understand that this was all part of my journey. God needed to strip away these distractions to prepare me for what He had in store, in His perfect timing—not mine. I had to reach the end of myself and truly trust in God's word, standing firm on His promises even when my eyes couldn't see the path ahead. I learned to embrace the truth that God is indeed the God of the impossible.

This journey has been incredibly tough, marked by countless tears, but it has taught me how to truly put God first, understand what love really means, and submit to His plans through obedience. Trusting Him when everything felt uncertain was a challenge, but it has strengthened my faith. Even as I write this, I'm still waiting on the promise, yet God has shifted my focus and filled me with a peace that surpasses all understanding (Philippians 4:6-7 NIV). I've found that contentment comes from nurturing my relationship with Him, leaning on prayer, and engaging with my community. I've learned to be at peace with God, regardless of whether the promise comes to pass. Once we reach that level of trust and surrender, we open ourselves to truly receive everything He has for us.

LET'S REFLECT

As you sit with the Holy Spirit, take a moment to reflect on these questions: If the promises you're holding onto never come to pass, will you still trust in God's goodness and faithfulness? When you feel weary in the waiting, how can you remind yourself of God's past faithfulness to help sustain your trust in His promises?

LET'S LISTEN

Take a moment with the scripture below to reflect and listen, inviting the Holy Spirit to guide you in your current situation. Come with an open heart and expect the unexpected.

"For no word from God will ever fail."

Luke 1:37 NIV

SCRIPTURE:

REFLECT:

LISTEN:

LET'S PRAY

Thank God for His limitless power. Ask Him to help you trust that nothing is impossible for Him, no matter the challenges you face.

DAY 26

HIS PURPOSE

Romans 8:28 CSB

At 26, I found myself really questioning my life and searching for my purpose. I wasn't walking with God and didn't know much about Him, but I had this strong feeling that He had spared my life for a reason. One day, as I was heading home from work like always, I suddenly felt faint—almost like I was in a déjà vu moment. Shortly after that, everything went black.

I woke up in an ambulance, still trying to figure out what had just happened. I didn't know where I was, and there were people around me asking simple questions that I couldn't answer. I couldn't even remember my own name. It's funny how in those moments, your mind goes blank, but I'll never forget what the doctor said first: "You should've been dead." That one line stuck with me and made me question why I was still alive. If God spared my life, what was the purpose behind it?

Once I regained my memory in the hospital, I found out that I'd had a seizure and flipped my car over a highway median. It's crazy, because I wasn't even on the highway. Thankfully, no one else was injured in the accident. After waiting six weeks to drive again, I got in the car and carried on with my life. My friends kept asking if I was nervous about getting back behind the wheel so soon, and I always reassured them I wasn't. Even in that moment, God was with me, reminding me that He didn't give us a spirit of fear (2 Timothy 1:7 CSB).

This was a defining moment for me. Looking back, I can see clearly how the enemy was trying to stop me before I even came to God. The devil knew the plans the Lord had for me. You'd think this experience would have drawn me closer to God, but it didn't; I continued on with my life. However, it did spark a desire for more. It reminded me that life is short, and I needed to make the most of the time I have left.

This accident awakened a passion in me to work with children, not only to teach them, but also to help them heal. I started researching careers and stumbled upon the field of occupational therapy in schools. I enrolled in school, and the rest is history. Even during my studies, God protected and provided for me in ways I never even thought to pray for. While my classmates struggled, God granted me a supernatural ease and grace, helping me excel and finish at the top of my class.

Throughout the Word, God tells us to trust in Him and assures us that He knows the plans He has for us (Jeremiah 29:11 CSB). The Lord leaves the 99 for the one, and little did I know I was that lost sheep. It took me another ten years to fully come back to Jesus, and He patiently waited, knowing all along that I would return.

In 2023, I attended a prophetic event where a man approached me and asked if something significant had happened to me at the age of 26. At first, I couldn't remember, as I've noticed that after the accident, some of my memories have been lost. As he continued to speak, he shared that my life was spared because God knew I would eventually come back to Him. He told me that the enemy could never take me out of God's hands again, and those words hit me deep.

To this day, I carry a small scar on my right hand from the accident. Someone told me it was because my body tensed up the way it did that I'm still here today. What's even more amazing is that a nurse friend of mine recently told me that most people who tense up similarly don't make it. My mind was blown! God works everything for our good, and looking back, I can see how even in the darkest moments, His hand was on me. If it weren't for that accident, I wouldn't have been pushed to change, grow, and ultimately return to Him.

So, if you're facing your own struggles or feeling uncertain, hold on to this: God sees you, He has a plan for you, and no matter how tough things get, He will never let you go. Your story isn't over yet. Keep trusting Him, because He's working everything out for your good!

LET'S REFLECT

As you sit with the Holy Spirit, take a moment to reflect on these questions: How can you see your struggles as part of God's bigger plan for your purpose? Are you willing to embrace the unknown, knowing that God has a purpose for every step you take?

LET'S LISTEN

Take a moment with the scripture below to reflect and listen, inviting the Holy Spirit to guide you in your current situation. Come with an open heart and expect the unexpected.

"We know that all things work together
for the good of those who love God,
who are called according to his purpose."

Romans 8:28 CSB

SCRIPTURE:

REFLECT:

LISTEN:

LET'S PRAY

Thank God for His promise to work everything together for your good. Ask Him to help you trust His plan, even when you can't see the whole picture.

DAY 27
HIS TEMPLE

1 Corinthians 6:19-20 NIV

Over the past year, the Lord has called me to do several Daniel fasts. If you're not familiar, a Daniel fast is a 21-day fast based on Daniel 10:3 NIV, where you only eat fruits, vegetables, and drink water. Honestly, every time I felt called to do it, I didn't want to! At first, I'd pray and ask God to confirm it because I wanted to be sure I was hearing Him right. But without fail, each time He confirmed it, I reluctantly went ahead and fasted.

The first week of the fast is always manageable, and I think, "Okay, I can do this!" But by week two, it's a whole different story. I start getting bored with the same brown rice and beans and begin craving an iced latte. It's a constant battle between my flesh and my spirit. As the word says, "The spirit is willing, but the flesh is weak" (Matthew 26:41 NIV). Every time I went through this, I realized it wasn't just about the foods I was denying myself—it was about truly connecting with God, learning to say no to my flesh, and seeking Him in moments of humility. There's a bigger purpose in all of this.

In the beginning, I focused on what I couldn't eat. I didn't realize that God was doing so much more—He was breaking things off of me and preparing me for something greater. With each passing day, as I drew near to Him, He drew near to me (James 4:8 NIV). I started hearing His voice more clearly. My faith, trust, and discernment were strengthened. I walked in His favor, became more sensitive to the Holy Spirit, and grew in obedience. It wasn't just about a change in diet; God was transforming me from the inside out. He knows that when we consume junk—whether physically or spiritually—we end up giving out junk. The enemy wants us so distracted, chewing on the ways of the world, that we are too full to consume the word of God.

When God gives us a word and our flesh immediately begins to fight it, do it! I learned that those are the moments that change us most dramatically. They stretch our faith and trust in God, making us ready to take the next radical step. Having faith doesn't make the process easy, but with God, it makes it possible. You never know what doors that small act of obedience might open. God will test us to see if we're ready for the blessings He wants to pour out on us (Deuteronomy 8:2-3 NIV). By heeding the instructions of the Lord, doors that I had been praying for opened at once, with this book as a bonus surprise.

Our bodies are His temple, and God wants us to honor Him with them. That means taking care of our physical health but also consuming the word of God. As Jesus said, "Man shall not live on bread alone, but on EVERY word that comes from the mouth of God" (Matthew 4:4 NIV). When we choose to live in obedience, we align ourselves with His will, and that's when transformation happens.

LET'S REFLECT

As you sit with the Holy Spirit, take a moment to reflect on these questions: In what areas of your life do you struggle to honor God with your body? When your flesh resists God's will, how can you strengthen your obedience and trust in His plan?

LET'S LISTEN

Take a moment with the scripture below to reflect and listen, inviting the Holy Spirit to guide you in your current situation. Come with an open heart and expect the unexpected.

"Do you not know that your bodies are temples of the Holy Spirit, who is in you, whom you have received from God? You are not your own; you were bought at a price. Therefore honor God with your bodies."

1 Corinthians 6:19-20 NIV

SCRIPTURE:

REFLECT:

LISTEN:

LET'S PRAY

Thank God for your body as His temple. Ask Him to help you honor Him with how you care for it.

DAY 28

FULL OF ANGER

Colossians 3:8 NIV

Growing up, I was angry. Looking at old pictures of myself, I discovered I rarely smiled as a kid. As I got older, I realized that I'd get mad over the smallest things, but the real issue was that I let that anger build up and turn into something worse—sin. The Bible says it's okay to be angry, but we shouldn't let it lead to sin or hold onto it (Ephesians 4:26 NIV). But that's exactly what I did. I didn't know how to express myself in a healthy way, so I bottled everything up until it exploded.

As a kid, I used to get back at people in small, spiteful ways—nothing that would hurt them physically, but enough to make them feel it. I'd make it look like it was their fault, and in my mind, that was how I got even. Honestly, I didn't understand where all that anger came from. I grew up in a home with a lot of yelling but no real room to express ourselves. I learned early that if you wanted your point to get across, you had to shout.

This mindset stuck with me and only got worse. Soon, I was yelling, cursing, and giving people the silent treatment in every situation. My road rage escalated quickly. I walked around with a scowl on my face, holding onto all that anger. The sad truth was, it was hurting me more than anyone else. I was so far gone that only Jesus could save me.

Coming to God was the best thing that ever happened to me. He knew the why behind my struggles even when I didn't. As I began to seek Him, His Word began to shine light on things I had buried deep inside. I spent so much of my life thinking that my anger was just a natural response, but I had deeper issues—spiritual strongholds the enemy used to keep me bound. These negative emotions weren't just the result of my upbringing; they were seeds planted by the enemy. Every time I held onto resentment, frustration, or unforgiveness, he fed them. Those spirits of anger silently took over parts of my heart and mind. I didn't even realize they were there until the Holy Spirit began revealing the darkness inside.

Often, we think of evil spirits as something external—like they possess people or attack from the outside. But sometimes they work from within, through unchecked emotions and thoughts. These spirits didn't just want me angry; they wanted to destroy me.

The change wasn't instant; it was a process of letting go of old patterns with God's grace. Once I understood the root of my anger (the lies urging me to hold grudges), I started to fight back. Through prayer and surrender, my relationship with Jesus helped me break free.

One of the most powerful moments in my healing came when I realized that forgiveness was key. Anger often feels justified, but when we hold onto it, we give the enemy a foothold. When I began to forgive (not just others, but myself), chains began to break. It was only through Christ that I could rid myself of that darkness. The more I drew near to Him, the more those spirits lost their hold.

I'm still learning to manage my emotions, but I don't carry that anger with me anymore. I don't curse, and I have a peace that surpasses all understanding. God is transforming me from the inside out, and by His grace, I'm becoming freer each day. If you're struggling with anger, rage, or any emotion that feels out of control, know this: You're not alone. Jesus understands our pain and has the power to break every chain.

LET'S REFLECT

As you sit with the Holy Spirit, take a moment to reflect on these questions: What negative behaviors or emotions do you struggle to release that might be holding you back spiritually? How do they affect your relationship with God and others?

LET'S LISTEN

Take a moment with the scripture below to reflect and listen, inviting the Holy Spirit to guide you in your current situation. Come with an open heart and expect the unexpected.

"But now you must also rid yourselves of all such things as these: anger, rage, malice, slander, and filthy language from your lips."

Colossians 3:8 NIV

SCRIPTURE:

REFLECT:

LISTEN:

LET'S PRAY

Ask God to show you any anger or bitterness in your heart, and invite Him to replace those with His peace and forgiveness.

DAY 29

SPIRIT OF FEAR

2 Timothy 1:7 NKJV

In 2015, when my Papa passed away, I attended my first funeral. I'd never seen a dead body before, let alone one I knew so well and so up-close. It was deeply painful to see my papa lying in that casket, but beneath the pain, I was filled with fear. At the end of the service, the family was given a chance to say their final goodbyes, and I remember walking up to the casket with my daddy, terrified to get too close. But my daddy, standing beside me, said something that stayed with me: "He's not going to hurt you." That was just enough to give me the courage to say goodbye. I reached out and touched his hand. It was so cold and lifeless, it brought tears to my eyes.

Later that night, as I lay in bed, those images haunted me. I started thinking about life and death—how one moment we're here, and the next, we're gone. My mind raced with all kinds of morbid thoughts, filling me with fear. I didn't realize it at the time, but I had unknowingly opened the door to the enemy. We're told not to give the enemy any opportunity

(Ephesians 4:27, NKJV), but my fear left the door wide open, and he slithered right in.

For the next few months, I was tormented by sleep paralysis. I was being spiritually attacked. When it happened, I couldn't move, but my mind was wide awake. Night after night, I'd hear strange noises and feel the presence of demonic spirits in my room. It got so intense that I even heard my name being called. But no matter how hard I tried, I didn't know what to do. I did everything I could think of to stop it, except calling on the name of Jesus.

At the time, I didn't know that Jesus' name is above every name and that at His name, every knee must bow (Philippians 2:10, 11 NKJV). I hadn't hidden God's Word in my heart, and I didn't know how to fight back against the devil's schemes. I felt helpless, trapped, and just took blow after blow.

I don't want that for you. Please, learn from my mistakes—call on the name of Jesus! There is power in His name. Build a prayer life. Dive into the Bible. When spiritual attacks come, you'll have scripture hidden in your heart, so that the Holy Spirit can bring it to your mind (John 14:26 NKJV). Remember, God promised to protect us in all ways (Psalm 91:11 NKJV). You can trust Him because He works all things for our good (Romans 8:28 NKJV). In Christ, you have authority and power to stand against any attack, and you can rest in the truth that we already have the victory in Him.

LET'S REFLECT

As you sit with the Holy Spirit, take a moment to reflect on these questions: When fear arises, do you lean on the Holy

Spirit or let the enemy's lies take control? How do you react to fear? Do you choose God's strength or let anxiety take over?

LET'S LISTEN

Take a moment with the scripture below to reflect and listen, inviting the Holy Spirit to guide you in your current situation. Come with an open heart and expect the unexpected.

"For God has not given us a spirit of fear,
but of power and of love and of a sound mind."

2 Timothy 1:7 NKJV

SCRIPTURE:

REFLECT:

LISTEN:

LET'S PRAY

Thank God for giving you a spirit of power, love, and a sound mind. Ask Him to help you recognize and resist fear, relying on His strength to walk boldly in His calling.

DAY 30
SEARCH ME

Psalm 139:23-24 NIV

The posture of your heart is the difference between surrendering to and giving up on God. When you surrender to God, you submit to Him and trust Him with your whole heart. You pray that His will be done in your life, no matter the outcome, because you understand that He knows what's best. Giving up on God is walking away, letting yourself be blown by the wind, showing Him that you have lost all faith, hope, and trust in the plans that He has for you.

The Word says that a double-minded man is unstable in all his ways (James 1:8 NIV), and that's what I was. I had to learn that my heart posture was my attitude, intentions, and my willingness to follow God. There were times in my life when I was given a promise and in a matter of a day, I'd go from standing on that word to doubting because I didn't SEE anything. How weak was that?

One day at church, the pastor delivered a powerful message on answered prayers that stood out to me. He highlighted three essential qualities needed for effective prayer: a surrendered heart, a righteous heart, and a faithful heart. It reminded me that the posture of our hearts is just as important as the words we pray when seeking God's answers.

Ask yourself: Why are you praying for that thing? Is it what God truly wants for you (Hebrews 5:7 NIV)? Are you living in righteousness, or is there unconfessed sin in your heart that might be keeping God from hearing you (Psalm 66:18 NIV)? And do you have a faithful heart that trusts in His Word? These questions hit me hard and made me reflect on my own heart, asking the Lord to search it. I don't want anything to stand in the way of my relationship with God or block my prayers from being heard.

Surrendering to God isn't a one-time decision—it's a daily decision. Let's be real: nothing worth having comes easy. I spent so much time trying to control things, forcing outcomes, and trying to make God's promises happen on my own. But in reality, all I did was make things harder. It's easy to think we know what's best, but God knows exactly what we need and when we're ready to receive. He's the one who sees the bigger picture.

The key is to let go of your expectations and trust Him fully. Surrender isn't about giving up; it's about giving God space to work. It's about releasing control and letting His will unfold in His perfect timing. When we trust Him, we open ourselves up to receive more than we could imagine. Surrendering may take time, but it's always worth it because God is faithful to fulfill His promises when our hearts are aligned with His. So let go, trust Him, and watch as He does what only He can do.

LET'S REFLECT

As you sit with the Holy Spirit, take a moment to reflect on these questions: Is your heart fully surrendered to God, or are you still holding on to control? Are you ready to let God search your heart, even if it means facing uncomfortable truths?

LET'S LISTEN

Take a moment with the scripture below to reflect and listen, inviting the Holy Spirit to guide you in your current situation. Come with an open heart and expect the unexpected.

"Search me, God, and know my heart;
test me and know my anxious thoughts.
See if there is any offensive way in me,
and lead me in the way everlasting."

Psalm 139:23-24 NIV

SCRIPTURE:

REFLECT:

LISTEN:

LET'S PRAY

Thank the Lord for His love and faithfulness. Ask Him to search your heart, reveal any sin or struggle, and guide you in His perfect will.

DAY 31
FAMILY WOUNDS

Ephesians 6:12-13 NLT

Growing up, my mama always told us, "What happens in this house stays in this house." As a child, it never bothered me. I followed the rules, spent time with my siblings and cousin, and I was good. But as I got older, I began to wonder why we didn't spend much time with family outside our house. Why were there never any family reunions, and why did we only gather with relatives I barely knew at funerals?

Something felt off, but it didn't hit me until I became the one on the outside looking in. After moving out, I started to feel disconnected, as if I wasn't truly part of the family. I was kept out of the loop, like my family was keeping a secret from me. I'd plan a trip to come visit, drive hours, and wasn't welcomed when I arrived. I felt pushed away and it left me so confused. I would compare my family to my friends' families. I realized how much more at home I felt in their houses than in my own. It got to a point when I came to visit, I found myself staying with friends or not visiting home at all. The loneliness grew, and a sense of abandonment took root in my heart.

I longed for a family of my own one day to fill the gap. The pain led me to take my frustrations out on the people I could see. It took time, but eventually, God showed me the truth: the hurt wasn't just about what was happening in the physical world—it was spiritual. There were wounds inside me that no person or relationship could heal. Only God could fill those empty spaces; only He could restore what had been broken.

I had spent so many years blaming my family for the pain I felt, not realizing there was a spiritual battle at play—one far beyond what I could see. The darkness in their lives and mine wasn't something I could fight with anger, frustration, or resentment. It was spiritual warfare that required spiritual weapons. God had to teach me how to fight in the spirit. I had to surrender my wounds to Him, trusting that only He could break the strongholds of darkness affecting my family for generations. It wasn't the people I needed to fight; it was the unseen forces of evil that had been working to divide and destroy.

As I learned to fight in prayer by putting on the full armor of God, I began to see a shift. The heaviness that once clouded my heart started to lift. I found healing, not by changing those around me, but by allowing God to change me and restore my perspective, my peace, and my ability to forgive. I realized that only through God's power I could break free from the lies, bitterness, and anger that had kept me trapped for so long.

In the end, the healing I longed for didn't come from fixing my family or my circumstances. It came from understanding the true source of my pain and learning to fight the right battle. God was my healer and protector, and in Him, I found the strength to break free.

LET'S REFLECT

As you sit with the Holy Spirit, take a moment to reflect on these questions: Are you facing spiritual battles with the weapons that truly matter? Are you trying to heal your pain by filling the emptiness with things that never truly satisfy you?

LET'S LISTEN

Take a moment with the scripture below to reflect and listen, inviting the Holy Spirit to guide you in your current situation. Come with an open heart and expect the unexpected.

"For we are not fighting against flesh-and-blood enemies, but against evil rulers and authorities of the unseen world, against mighty powers in this dark world, and against evil spirits in the heavenly places. Therefore, put on every piece of God's armor so you will be able to resist the enemy in the time of evil. Then after the battle you will still be standing firm."

Ephesians 6:12-13 NLT

SCRIPTURE:

REFLECT:

LISTEN:

LET'S PRAY

Thank the Lord for equipping you with His armor. Ask Him to reveal any areas where you're relying on your own strength instead of His. Pray for the wisdom to fight spiritual battles with the right weapons, standing firm in His power and truth.

DAY 32
SHINE BRIGHT

Matthew 5:16 NIV

This morning, getting out of bed was a struggle. I was tired! But I pushed through and got dressed for the day. In a rush to leave the house, I prayed to God, asking Him to let the day go as He planned, to protect me and give me His peace. I arrived at work, and the test began.

For one, I was exhausted! I'd made my coffee with three shots of espresso, but I couldn't even take a sip! I got to my office, and for a second, it was peaceful. Then I saw a missed call from my boss about a meeting. As that was happening, people were knocking at my door with questions flying at me from all sides! Then I was irritated.

Then came the final blow. There was no other room in the entire school for testing except my office, and per state rules, I couldn't be in there! My flesh was ready to take over, and I was about to let it.

I was barely functioning on little sleep, and my office was filled with everything I needed for my client sessions, but I couldn't even access them. For a moment, I thought, Why am I even at work today? I was so annoyed, and my frustration slipped out. Thankfully, I have a relationship with Jesus. I was immediately convicted and asked the Holy Spirit for help.

We know we're supposed to let God's light shine through us in moments like these, but do we really? The enemy is always looking for a crack to slip through, and if we're not careful, staying in that frustrated space too long can lead to sin. The more we sit in it, the further we feel from Jesus. But here's the truth: You're never too far gone to come back home.

I prayed until I felt God's peace settle in. I asked Him to help me guard my words, knowing that harsh words only stir up more anger (Proverbs 15:1). I had to release control and choose not to let this situation offend me, but instead focus on the positive. I thanked God for shifting my perspective, reminding me that in an hour or two, I would have my space back (1 Thessalonians 5:18). A few years ago, I would've let the enemy take my whole day. Thank God for wisdom!

God knows how He made us. We all have our moments, and things will trigger us. The key is not to stay stuck in it, but to bring it to Him because He cares (1 Peter 5:7 NIV). We were never meant to carry heavy burdens. It's moments like these, where we feel tested, that God uses to grow the good fruit in us (Galatians 5:22-23 NIV). Until we pass the test of choosing the fruit of the Spirit over our flesh, we'll keep facing the same test.

Living in a way that lets your light shine means reflecting God's love, truth, and goodness in all areas of your life. When others see our good deeds, they should be pointed to the One who enables us to live that way—God. And in doing so, they will glorify Him. In moments like this, we're reminded that no matter how frustrated we get, God is always ready to help us reset. We just need to turn to Him, choose peace, and let His light shine, even when our flesh wants to take over.

LET'S REFLECT

As you sit with the Holy Spirit, take a moment to reflect on these questions: When frustration or anger arises, do you surrender it to God or let it control you? When the Holy Spirit convicts you, do you repent or justify your actions?

LET'S LISTEN

Take a moment with the scripture below to reflect and listen, inviting the Holy Spirit to guide you in your current situation. Come with an open heart and expect the unexpected.

"In the same way, let your light shine before others, that they may see your good deeds and glorify your Father in heaven."

Matthew 5:16 NIV

SCRIPTURE:

REFLECT:

LISTEN:

LET'S PRAY

Thank the Lord for His guidance and the opportunity to reflect His light. Ask Him to help you shine brightly in all you do, so that others may see His goodness and glorify Him.

DAY 33

MY BEST FRIEND

John 15:15 NIV

My relationship with Jesus is incredibly important to me. Just like any relationship, it requires effort and intentionality to grow. The Word says that when we draw near to God, He draws near to us (James 4:8 NIV). God longs for a close relationship with us, but He won't force Himself on us. Instead, He responds when we seek Him with a sincere heart.

In 2022, Jesus became my best friend. I found myself in a season of isolation, but at the time, I didn't understand why. I only knew all the people who were close to me were leaving. With confusion setting in, I ran to God for answers.

Spending time with Jesus made me realize that He allowed certain relationships to end because He needed my full attention for what He was about to do in my life. It was a season for change, and unfortunately, not everyone could go. During that time, all I had was Jesus. I learned to trust Him completely, to seek Him with all my heart, and be fully led by the Holy Spirit.

Jesus showed me what it truly means to hear His voice and follow His lead. He equipped me for the calling He placed on my life long before I was born (Jeremiah 1:5 NIV). That year, He led me to an amazing church and taught me how to truly sit at His feet, finding contentment in Him alone. With everything shifting in my life, I knew it was the right moment to be baptized, publicly committing and rededicating myself to my Lord and Savior.

With God not yet allowing the door to be fully opened to others, I talked to Jesus about everything! There were moments of tears and laughter, and times when the impossible became possible, experiences I'll never forget. In every situation, God showed up, straightening every crooked path. And because I shared my heart with Jesus, He revealed things I never would have known otherwise.

Time and time again, God has proven Himself to be my protector and provider, the one I can always trust. Even when things didn't look the way He promised, He reminded me to walk by faith (2 Corinthians 5:7 NIV). I can honestly say that I am in love with Jesus, and I never want to be without Him.

If this resonates with your heart, start by talking to Jesus. Share with Him everything you would tell your closest friends. Spend time with Him daily, include Him in everything you do, and acknowledge Him; He'll guide your steps (Proverbs 3:6 NIV). Remember, He is always with you, loves you unconditionally, and understands you more deeply than anyone else ever could. Let His peace and presence be enough for you.

LET'S REFLECT

As you sit with the Holy Spirit, take a moment to reflect on these questions: What does it mean to you personally that Jesus calls you His friend, rather than just a servant? How can you build a deeper, more personal relationship with Jesus daily? How can you reflect Jesus' love and truth to others, showing them the friendship He offers?

LET'S LISTEN

Take a moment with the scripture below to reflect and listen, inviting the Holy Spirit to guide you in your current situation. Come with an open heart and expect the unexpected.

"I no longer call you servants, because a servant does not know his master's business. Instead, I have called you friends, for everything that I learned from my Father I have made known to you."

John 15:15 NIV

SCRIPTURE:

REFLECT:

LISTEN:

LET'S PRAY

Thank Jesus for calling you His friend. Ask Him to help you grow closer to Him and reflect His love to others, so they may know His friendship too.

DAY 34
BE REAL

James 5:16 NIV

Writing this book was an incredibly personal journey—one that I didn't expect to be so challenging. Every single day, I would sit down at my computer, asking God what He wanted me to write, seeking His guidance on every word. It wasn't just about sharing my story; it was about trusting God to reveal what He wanted to use through my pain to help others heal. Knowing that whoever reads it will draw closer to Him, I wanted His Spirit to guide every page.

I had to surrender completely to God throughout the process, and honestly, that surrender made me uncomfortable. It made me feel vulnerable, exposed—like I was standing naked before the world. As I wrote, I found myself sharing things I had never even told my closest friends or family. It was like I was peeling back layers of pain I'd kept hidden for so long. I struggled in silence for years, and only Jesus truly knew the depth of the emotions I carried. He was the one who saw my heart and understood the silent battles I fought.

I remember days when I'd sit at my desk, praying for God to help me write, unsure of how to even begin. There were moments when the words didn't come easily, and I felt stuck. But then, there were other days when it flowed—when the Holy Spirit just moved through me, and I knew exactly what to say. It was in those moments that I realized this book was as much for me as it was for anyone else. Writing it became an act of healing. It was the final step in truly confronting and letting go of the pain from my past.

Through this process, I learned that healing isn't just about the past being behind us; it's about letting God work through us in the present. Sharing our stories, even the painful ones, allows God to use our experiences to heal others, and in turn, it heals us too. It's as though the more we give, the more He fills us with His peace. I encourage anyone who's struggling to open themselves up to God and let Him take control of the healing process. It's not easy. It requires vulnerability, patience, and trust. But when we allow Him to work in us, He can take even the most broken parts and transform them into something beautiful.

Allow God to lead you through your healing. Spend time in prayer, asking Him to help you confront the hurt that still lingers. Be open to His guidance and trust that He knows exactly what needs to be revealed. Don't rush the process; healing takes time. Let God show you the beauty that can come from your pain and the strength you can find in your surrender. As you allow Him to do the work, He will not only heal you but also equip you to share your testimony with others, helping them heal as well.

LET'S REFLECT

As you sit with the Holy Spirit, take a moment to reflect on these questions: How can sharing your struggles and praying for others lead to healing for both them and yourself? In what ways can being vulnerable with others allow you to experience God's healing power?

LET'S LISTEN

Take a moment with the scripture below to reflect and listen, inviting the Holy Spirit to guide you in your current situation. Come with an open heart and expect the unexpected.

"Therefore confess your sins to each other and pray for each other so that you may be healed. The prayer of a righteous person is powerful and effective."

James 5:16 NIV

SCRIPTURE:

REFLECT:

LISTEN:

LET'S PRAY

Thank the Lord for the power of prayer and the healing it brings. Ask Him to help you be open and vulnerable with others, so that His peace and restoration can flow through you.

DAY 35
MOTHERHOOD UNFOLDING

James 1:4 NKJV

I've always had this burning desire to be a mom, and if I'm honest, I've always pictured myself with a little boy. I would pray, asking God to prepare me for that season. I wanted God to bring my child into my life when I was truly ready, not just to nurture him, but when I had become the best version of myself. I wanted to experience growth, healing, and self-care before stepping into the calling of motherhood.

As the years passed and I still didn't have children, I started to realize something important: I had waited this long for a reason. I knew I wanted to do things the right way, to trust God's perfect timing and surrender my plans to Him. I learned that with every promise from God, there's always a waiting season, and in that waiting, He's working to prepare you for what you've been praying for. You may not always see how or when, but you have to trust that He's shaping you in ways you can't yet understand. Trust the process.

Trusting the process and actually walking it out are two very different things, and let me tell you, it's easier said than done! There were moments when my patience wore thin, and I found myself wanting this waiting season to hurry up and end. But then, something unexpected happened. God began to open doors to divine friendships, and I started noticing a pattern. Every woman I connected with over the past few years was a mom to a little boy. Little did I know, that was the beginning of my preparation season.

Spending time with these women, I saw the raw side of motherhood, sleepless nights, endless responsibilities, and the constant struggle to balance it all. What stood out wasn't just the challenges, but the love. The pure, unconditional love they poured into their kids, even when they were running on empty.

I realized this was exactly what I had been praying for, not just a son, but understanding the sacrifice, strength, and grace that come with motherhood. God allowed these women to show me the beauty in the struggle, but the joy in the journey. Seeing this made me truly appreciate the season I'm in. I have the freedom to focus only on growth and self-care, knowing that when the time was right, God would make it happen.

Looking back, I can see how every friendship, every lesson, and every moment was shaping me. God wasn't just preparing me with time; He was using the people and experiences He placed in my life to mold me. I'm so grateful to God for opening my eyes to see how each person He brought into my life has played a part in shaping me into the mother He's called me to be.

LET'S REFLECT

As you sit with the Holy Spirit, take a moment to reflect on these questions: How do you trust God's timing when you're waiting? Are you able to see how God is preparing you during the waiting season? What if the "delay" is God's way of preparing you?

LET'S LISTEN

Take a moment with the scripture below to reflect and listen, inviting the Holy Spirit to guide you in your current situation. Come with an open heart and expect the unexpected.

"But let patience have its perfect work, that you may be perfect and complete, lacking nothing."

James 1:4 NKJV

SCRIPTURE:

REFLECT:

LISTEN:

LET'S PRAY

Thank God for the growth that comes through waiting. Ask Him to help you trust His timing and embrace the process, knowing He is shaping you into who He wants you to be.

DAY 36
GOD KNOWS THE PLANS

Jeremiah 29:11 NIV

I love the woman God has made me over these last few years, and the best part is that I know He isn't done. I can look back and see how God has truly made me a new creation in Christ (2 Corinthians 5:17 NIV). I am at a point in my journey where I understand that He knows what tomorrow brings, and that I can trust Him with every detail.

Throughout this journey, I've struggled with trusting God's timing. I found it hard to surrender everything to Him because I was used to being in control. I battled with double-mindedness regarding the promises He gave me and often forgot that He is the God of the impossible, the same God who spoke the world into existence with just His voice.

God didn't give us the Bible just to read; He gave us His Word to believe, to live by, and to use as a daily guide. No matter what we're facing, the Bible has scripture that speaks directly to our situation. God calls us to pick up our cross and walk, to follow Him, and to walk by faith. If we knew every step of the plan God has for us, why would we need to trust

Him or walk by faith? Walking by faith means trusting that God has the bigger picture in mind, even when we can't see it yet.

My walk with the Lord has really opened my eyes to who He is, and that's where everything begins. Knowing His character and understanding how He loves us has completely changed the way that I read His Word. In it, He promised to be our protector, our provider, and guide, showing us the way forward. Only the One with the plans can do that! All we need to do is listen, trust, and obey, and He's got us.

Reflecting on my journey, I'm amazed at how God has transformed me. His love, timing, and plans are more than I ever hoped for. Trusting Him with every detail of my life has been a process, but I've learned that His way is always better than mine. If you're wondering if God can truly change your life, I can tell you from experience: He can. God's promises are true, and His Word is what guides us. We don't need to know every step of the plan.

So, let go of the fear and pressure to have it all figured out. Surrender to the One who loves you and has a perfect plan for you. Trust Him. He's got you.

LET'S REFLECT

As you sit with the Holy Spirit, take a moment to reflect on these questions: How can you trust that God's plans for you are better than your own? How can you remind yourself that God's plan for your life is filled with hope and a future, even when things don't go as expected?

LET'S LISTEN

Take a moment with the scripture below to reflect and listen, inviting the Holy Spirit to guide you in your current situation. Come with an open heart and expect the unexpected.

"For I know the plans I have for you," declares the Lord, "plans to prosper you and not to harm you, plans to give you a hope and a future."

Jeremiah 29:11 NIV

SCRIPTURE:

REFLECT:

LISTEN:

LET'S PRAY

Thank God for His plans to prosper you and give you a hope and a future. Ask Him to help you trust His timing and embrace the process, knowing that He is guiding you toward His good and perfect purpose.

ABOUT THE AUTHOR

Erika Hartfield is an occupational therapy practitioner in the school system and an ordained minister. At 36, she surrendered her life to God, and He completely transformed her journey, leading her from Atlanta, Georgia, to North Carolina, where she now lives and serves with a heart fully devoted to Him. She is passionate about helping others heal, grow, and learn to hear God's voice for themselves. Her background in therapy has given her a deep compassion for both spiritual and emotional healing, and she delights in walking alongside others on their own journeys.

This book was written through prayer and obedience, trusting the Holy Spirit to guide every word. Erika is also preparing to launch All Ears Ministries, a Spirit-led teaching and coaching ministry designed to help believers grow closer to God and discern His voice with confidence.

www.ingramcontent.com/pod-product-compliance
Lightning Source LLC
La Vergne TN
LVHW010102110826
845155LV00028B/446